Live Growth Focused Kid Edition

How to Excel in Life with a Growth Mindset

Dr. Michelle Ihrig

Live Growth Focused Kid Edition: How to Excel in Life with a Growth Mindset
© 2022 by Dr. Michelle Ihrig. All Rights Reserved.

All rights reserved. No part of this book may be reproduced in any form or by any electronic or mechanical means including information storage and retrieval systems, without permission in writing from the author. The only exception is by a reviewer, who may quote short excerpts in a review.

Cover designed by Dr. Michelle Ihrig

Special thanks to the following envato elements designers:
aHandDrawn
betoalanis
ddraw
iconbunny
iconsoul
jumsoft
Middtone
and especially: wowomnom

Live Growth Focused
www.LiveGrowthFocused.com

Printed in the United States of America

First Printing: July 2022
Live Growth Focused

ISBN-13 978-1-946568-47-2

I dedicate this book
to my students

Growth Mindset:

Always do your best,

even when it is hard.

CONTENTS

Hi! – An Introduction	p.1
1. Because We Grow	p.5
2. Remember the Good Story	p.13
3. School	p.22
4. Friends	p.30
5. Screen Time	p.37
6. Being Part of a Team	p.47
7. Grown-Ups	p.54
8. Who Am I?	p.63
9. This is Me	p.70
10. Foundations	p.82
11. Now What?	p.92
Action Steps	p.105
Doodle Pages	p.109
About the Author	p.115

Live Growth Focused Kid Edition

Hi!

My name is Doc Chelle.

I am a teacher.

In this book, I will help you believe in yourself by teaching you about having a growth mindset.

You can have a growth mindset in many places like music, art, science, technology, and sports.

Dr. Michelle Ihrig

Sometimes people talk about the pretend elephant in the room when they do not want to talk about something important.

The pretend elephant we are going to talk about is why should you read and color in this book when
you could be doing
something else?

Live Growth Focused Kid Edition

The answer is because unlike some of the games you play or the shows you watch, what you learn in this book can help you to become a BETTER YOU!

There are reflection questions for you to think about at the end of each chapter.

You can draw or write your answers…actually, you can do both!

Even if you only learn one new thing, your life could be better in that one area, which is a good thing!

Talk soon! Doc Chelle.

Chapter 1
Because We Grow

Before you were born, Dr. Carol Dweck wrote about two different kinds of mindsets:

Fixed Mindset   and   Growth Mindset.

A person with a fixed mindset says things like this....
I can't do this.
I'll never get better.
Why should I try?

Live Growth Focused Kid Edition

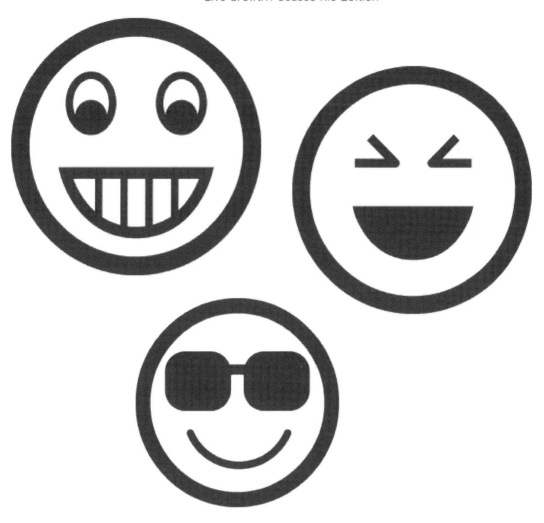

A person with a growth mindset says the opposite...
I can do this!
It is okay; I will try again.
What can I do differently?

 One student said a fixed mindset was "a kind of poison for the brain."

The student said a growth mindset was "like medicine for the brain."

When you decide to use a growth mindset, your whole world could change. You will learn new things and become the best version of yourself!

I can choose to have a growth mindset.

Reflection #1

Describe a person with fixed mindset and a person with a growth mindset.

Fixed Mindset	Growth Mindset

Reflection #2

Where do you want to use a growth mindset?

Chapter 2
Remember the Good Story

Life can be hard at times. Sometimes, we feel sad or upset, and that is okay.

A growth focused person thinks about the difficult time and then thinks about what good can come from it.

Years ago, I lived in another country away from my family and my friends. Sometimes, I felt sad.

Soon, I loved my new home.
I made new friends, and I started a new job helping people.

Almost every week, I would walk by the beach, and several orphaned dogs would come to visit my yard for food.

 When I moved back home, I wrote a book about some of the animals I met.

Instead of remembering the hard times, I chose to think about the happier times. What are your happy memories?

Eating ice cream or going swimming?

What about camping or riding on a scooter?

Or learning to play an instrument or building with Legos?

When we learn from our mistakes, then we can write our good story.

It is time for you to tell your good story and to shine like the brightest star!

Live Growth Focused Kid Edition

When we learn, we grow.

Dr. Michelle Ihrig

Reflection #3

Describe someone who struggled and still had a good story. It can be a Disney character, another cartoon, or someone in real life.

Live Growth Focused Kid Edition

Reflection #4

When was a time you overcame something difficult? How did it make you feel?

Dr. Michelle Ihrig

Chapter 3

School

Some kids like going to school to learn.

Some kids like going to school to play or to be with friends.

Sometimes you will like going to school, and sometimes you will not want to go.

I like to learn. I read all the time, and I enjoy working on math problems.

But, at school, I did not ask many questions.
I did not always try to do my best.

I had a fixed mindset.

When you are in school, asking questions and asking for help are examples of having a growth mindset.

You might raise your hand to ask your teacher. Perhaps you might turn and talk with a neighbor during small groups to get help.

At home, you might even watch a YouTube video to learn more.

I often tell my students I want their brains to hurt in class because they are thinking so much and working so hard.

A growth mindset means doing my best, even if it is hard.

Dr. Michelle Ihrig

Reflection #5

When is it hard for you to do your best?

Reflection #6

How do you act when you are doing your best?

Chapter 4

Friends

For some kids, making friends is easy. For other kids, making friends can be difficult.

As you grow up, your interests may change.

Maybe when you were younger, you liked dinosaurs, but as you got older, perhaps you became interested in art or sports.

The important thing is for you to be true to you.

Do not change because someone else wants you to change.

There will be people you like, and sometimes there will be people you do not like.

That is okay!

The important thing is to treat everyone kindly no matter what.

Another important thing is always to feel safe.

If someone hurts you or is mean to you, get help! Your teacher, your parents, or any grown-up can help.

Dr. Michelle Ihrig

We all want you to be successful and live long happy lives.

Please,
Be a friend,
not a bully.

Live Growth Focused Kid Edition

Reflection #7

Who is someone who helps you do your best?

How do they help you?

Dr. Michelle Ihrig

Reflection #8

How can you be more helpful to others?

Live Growth Focused Kid Edition

Chapter 5

Some kids spend a lot of time using technology for enjoyment.

They may use a phone, computer, game system, or tablet.

Maybe you watch YouTube, play games, or make videos.

When I was younger, we did not have computers,

cell phones, or Kindles.

Instead, we had typewriters, corded phones, and books!

We did not have on demand shows which you may watch on Netflix, Amazon Prime, Disney+, and YouTube.

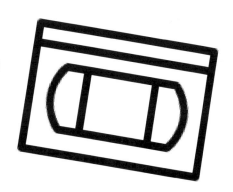

We watched what was on TV or drove to a store or to the library to borrow a movie to watch.

Usually, we did other activities. We might read, go bowling, or play outside.

 In 2018, kids spent an average of almost six hours using entertainment a day.

 Some kids listened to music, some kids played games, others watched videos online, and some did all three at once!

At times, I overuse technology, too. Years ago, I played one game about cooking for over an hour a day!

Sometimes, I binge watch five episodes of a show in a row!

Too much screen time can be bad. It can hinder your creativity. It can make you lazy. It could even affect your eyes.

There are times you will need technology to learn. For example, my YouTube channel ProdigyHelp.com teaches kids math.

A growth focused person creates balance.

You should spend time on technology learning and a smaller amount of time playing.

Just remember to take breaks from technology. You could read a book, draw, or play outside. Your brain will appreciate the time away!

Dr. Michelle Ihrig

LOVE YOURSELF and UNPLUG!

Reflection #9

Make a list of how you use technology in a week.

Entertainment/Fun Uses	Productive/Learning Uses

Dr. Michelle Ihrig

Reflection #10

What are five ways you can use technology productively when your parents give you screen time?

Chapter 6

Being Part of a Team

Most likely, you have already been part of a team. Maybe you play a sport, or you were on a team during gym class.

Maybe your teacher asked you to work with other classmates on an assignment.

Maybe you participate in drama, are on a computer team, are in scouts, or are involved with another activity where you work with other people.

Group activities teach us qualities called soft skills that we cannot learn alone.

Some examples include communication, collaboration, and fair play.

One of my students said using a growth mindset helped her with swimming by focusing on improving her time. She said: "I also use it in relays when I race with my teammates."

Being on a team helps you learn to support and to help others while you learn to accept help.

One student said a growth mindset helped him to "try and become a better player but also work on being the best teammate I can be, by showing up to all the practices and trying my hardest every practice, not just for myself but also for my teammates."

Growth mindset is about becoming your best with the help of others.

Dr. Michelle Ihrig

Reflection #11

What teams or groups are you part of?

What do you like about them?

Reflection #12

Describe the qualities you believe would make a good team.

Dr. Michelle Ihrig

Chapter 7

Grown-Ups

Because you are a kid, you likely have many grown-ups in your life: your family, your teacher, maybe even your bus driver.

Sometimes, kids and adults understand each other very easily…and sometimes we struggle.

One of my students talked about how much fun she had with her family.

When she got older, they had more arguments. She said one of the things they argued the most about was her cleaning her room and helping with chores.

She decided to come up with a plan.

 She started by simply cleaning her room. Then, she helped out more.

Soon, her parents noticed a change.

My student said,
"I grew as a person,
a daughter, and a sister,
and not only did I see my
growth, so did others."

It is important to remember that sometimes change takes time.

If you ever feel sad,
overwhelmed, or
frustrated,
you must talk to
someone about it.

Hopefully, you can talk to your parents. You can also talk to your teachers, your principal, even the custodian at school.

If the adult does not know how to help you, they will find someone who can.

We all need people to help us on our journeys.

Reflection #13

Which adults in your life do you sometimes struggle talking to? Why? What can you do to make it better?

Reflection #14

Which adults do you trust and talk to when you need help? Why? Which other adults can you ask for help?

Chapter 8
Who Am I?

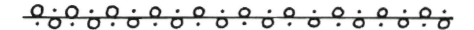

Being a kid can be challenging. You have responsibilities like homework, nightly reading, helping at home, maybe even making your own snack, or assisting with dinner.

Now is the time when you will start to discover your interests. What do you like? What do you not like?
What makes you happy?
Who makes you happy?

You will also start making friendships. Some friendships may last a long time, and others may last only a few days.

As you get older, your interests change, and that is okay!

 Maybe you liked trains, and now you like computers.

Maybe you liked to sing, and now you like to read.

 The same is true at school.

The more you understand and share how you like to learn best, the more your teachers can help you.

It is okay to get help as you become your best.

Reflection #15

Make a list of your best qualities.

Are you kind? giving? honest?

Live Growth Focused Kid Edition

Reflection #16

Who helps you to become your absolute best?

Chapter 9
This Is Me

Once you discovered who you are, it is time to stay true to who you are.

Sometimes, you might face peer pressure. This happens when you want to do one thing, and your friends or classmates want to do something else.

Here are some examples:

Your teacher placed you in a group. Two of your classmates at the table want to talk instead. What do you do?

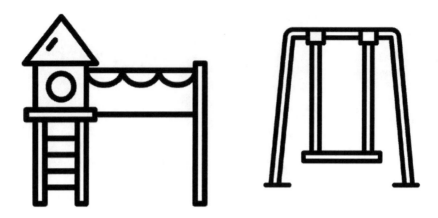

You are at the playground during recess. You see someone being unkind to someone else. What do you do?

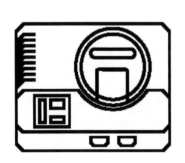

You go to a friend's house. They want you to play a video game that you know your parents would not want you playing. What do you do?

 When you face peer pressure, it can be hard to be true to you.

It is also the most critical time for you to have a growth mindset and stand up for what you believe and for what you want.

One summer I returned to school and saw one of my students in the parking lot. He was at school because he was in the marching band.

I could tell that made him incredibly happy.

Some people may not think marching band is a worthwhile activity. My student did not care. He  stayed true to what made him happy, he worked hard, and it showed.

 Another one of my students wanted to be a better artist.

She was not a good artist at first, but she worked hard to practice drawing and painting every day.

She told me, "I just recently became satisfied with my artwork. I felt accomplished and empowered."

 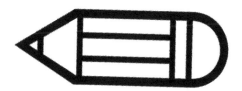

She thought someone with natural talent may not appreciate their artwork as much as she appreciates hers because she worked hard to become the artist she is today.

 People with a growth mindset want to improve, so they usually like advice.

Living growth focused means working to be your best, taking feedback when needed, and asking for help.

You are too important to be anyone else but yourself. Please, Be True to You!

Dr. Michelle Ihrig

Reflection #17

What qualities do you like about yourself?

What areas can you improve?

Things I like about me:	Things I want to improve:

Reflection #18

When was a time you had to make a hard choice?

What happened?

Dr. Michelle Ihrig

Chapter 10

Foundations

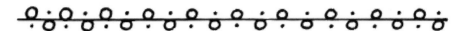

Over the past nine chapters,
we learned about how to
live growth focused
at school, with friends,
at home, and on teams.

Now we are going to talk about
creating a foundation
for the future.

Think of it like a set of rules
that you write for yourself
to help you be a good person.

Here are some of

the guidelines I follow:

Everyone can bring happiness. Sometimes they may choose to bring sadness, and I cannot force them to change that.

Integrity matters – there is power in words and actions, and living an honest life is possible.

Life is a process – I do not have all the answers.

What I think today could be different tomorrow based on new information and experiences,

and that is okay.

Forgiveness, while occasionally painful at first, is important.

Parents and caregivers should be respected, even when I think they may not deserve it or it may be challenging for me.

Finally, we are interdependent, and we need each other.

These are some of the guidelines that I follow in my life.

The choices I make, the actions I take, the words I speak, the places I go, etc. are all considered through my desire to be a good person.

What you say
and
what you do
matters.

Dr. Michelle Ihrig

Reflection #19

What rules or guidelines do you follow for your life?

Reflection #20

Who can help you to be a good person?

Chapter 11

Now What?

Congratulations!

You almost read the entire book!

Now, we are going to review some of the major topics we covered.

After each statement,

draw a picture or write a short journal entry about the statement or thought at the top of the page.

Maybe you will reflect about the thought itself, and maybe you will connect it to your life and how you will use it in the future.

#1: Living growth focused is a good thing!

A growth focused person looks at circumstances as opportunities to grow. The opposite of a growth mindset is a fixed mindset; those people are stuck in their circumstances.

#2: It is important to write our own stories. Instead of focusing on the bad or hard times, we should remember happier times and strive to learn from the difficult times to become better.

#3: At school, we should always try to be our best, even when it is challenging. It is okay to make mistakes and to ask for help if we are trying to be better.

#4: Some people in our lives help us to be better people, and other people may end up making us sad. The important thing is to grow from the good and from the challenging.

#5: We need to live a balanced life. Although there are benefits in using technology, we should be mindful in how we spend our time.

#6: Being part of a team is important because we can learn skills which we might not learn elsewhere.

#7: Grown-ups want to help us to become better. We should seek their help when we need it – even when we do not want to.

#8: Part of growing up is learning about who we are, what we like, what are our strengths, and what areas we need to improve in.

#9: Once we determine who we are, then it is important to stay true to ourselves and not change because of pressure from other people.

Dr. Michelle Ihrig

#10: Laying a foundation for the future helps us live with integrity.

Now that you have reflected on some of the core concepts of the book, it is time to put a plan in place for you to Live Growth Focused.

I suggest starting small and focusing on one area of your life first.

Here are some examples:

Doing better at school
Getting along with your siblings
Cleaning your room
Working on a new activity
Using technology less

Once you decide what area you want to improve, then you will need to come up with a goal and a plan of action. The following pages will help you.

Once you start to take a few steps, then take a few more steps. Then, add start improving in another area.

The power to Live Growth Focused is in your hands!

I believe in YOU.

With love,
Doc Chelle

Live Growth Focused Kid Edition

Action Plan #1

Which area did you select?

What is your goal?

What are three steps you can take to improve in this area?

Whom can you ask to help you improve?

Dr. Michelle Ihrig

Action Plan #2

Which area did you select?

What is your goal?

What are three steps you can take to improve in this area?

Whom can you ask to help you improve?

Action Plan #3

Which area did you select?

What is your goal?

What are three steps you can take to improve in this area?

Whom can you ask to help you improve?

Dr. Michelle Ihrig

Action Plan #4

Which area did you select?

What is your goal?

What are three steps you can take to improve in this area?

Whom can you ask to help you improve?

Live Growth Focused Kid Edition

Doodle Page

Dr. Michelle Ihrig

Doodle Page

Doodle Page

Dr. Michelle Ihrig

Doodle Page

Live Growth Focused Kid Edition

Doodle Page

Dr. Michelle Ihrig

Doodle Page

About the Author

Dr. Michelle Ihrig is an author/educator based in Atlanta, Georgia. Her gift is the ability to see the greatness in people and to provide them with the tools, resources, and motivation needed to strategically work and to truly shine.

Dr. Ihrig is a certified educator in Mathematics, Special Education, English as an Additional Language, Gifted Education, Online Education, and Administration. Her doctoral focus was best practices of inclusive education at international schools.

Dr. Ihrig is also the author of Scripture Life Devotionals and Black Bear Coloring Literacy Books.

Made in the USA
Columbia, SC
10 July 2022